FLOWING FROM WITHIN

Finding Hope in and Feeling the Presence of God

A 21-DAY DEVOTIONAL

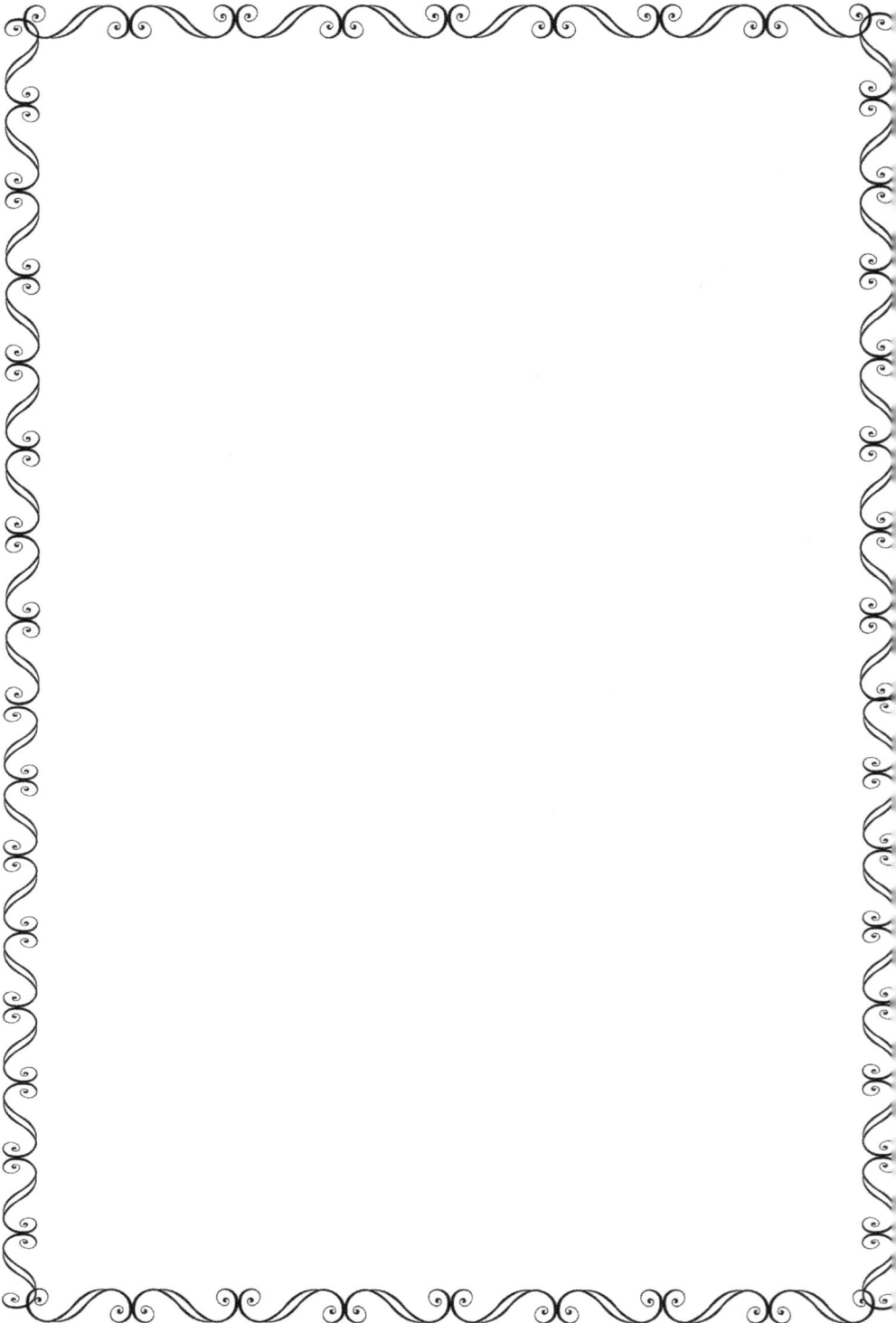

FLOWING FROM WITHIN

Finding Hope in and Feeling the Presence of God

A 21-DAY DEVOTIONAL

TERUCO F. TYNES CHARLES

Manufactured in the United States of America.

ISBN: 979-8-9909350-4-4 First Edition USA $17.99.

*All Scripture references in this book are from the Holy Bible, utilizing
three versions: King James Version (KJV), New International Version
(NIV), and the New Revised Standard Version Updated Edition
(NRSVUE). All Scripture has been sourced from BibleGateway.com.*

THIS GIFT IS FOR:

_____

FROM:

_____

DATE:

_____

Acknowledgements

For your unwavering support, constant love, and

much appreciated prayers,

to

my husband Surish

and

daughter Ari.

Dedication

It is my humble honour to dedicate this book to
you for all

the love, care, and examples of genuine, pure, active faith.

What you have poured into me over the years,

I will forever carry it in my heart.

In Loving Memory:

Mummy Belle (grandaunt)

and

Donavon Sr.

Table of Contents

Introduction

Putting pen to paper to create a book has been a personal goal of mine for quite some time. As other aspects of life took priority, the dream was increasingly pushed further to the peripherals.

During the pandemic of the early 2020s, both the harsh reality and fragility of life hit home. Apprehensive about departing this life without having a formal record of my thoughts, I was prompted to make a concerted effort to bring my dream to fruition.

I genuinely believe that daily interactions with Yahweh are necessary to yield life-altering results. Deliberate daily moments with the Divine are impactful as they offer me the hope, encouragement, and confidence I need to face challenges. Such time brings to life a deeper understanding of the Author's words in Lamentations,

---

Lamentations 3:21 - 23, NRSVUE, [21] *"But this I call to mind, and therefore I have hope:* [22] *The steadfast love of the LORD never ceases, his mercies never come to an end;* [23] *they are new every morning; great is your faithfulness."*

In writing this book, I aim to provide an impactful, user-friendly devotional. The upcoming pages include a format I believe is simple to follow and engage with. Each of the 21 days begins with a purposefully selected Opening Scripture from the Holy Bible, of which two versions are utilised, New International (NIV) and New Revised Standard Version Updated Edition (NRSVUE). All Scripture is sourced from Biblegateway.com.

Following the Opening Scripture are words of reflection that I hope will resonate with you. I sometimes include or reference Scripture from the King James Version (KJV), NIV, and NRSVUE.

At a very young age, I was welcomed into the home of my maternal grandaunt. A deep relationship evolved, so I affectionately refer to her as "Mummy." She is referenced this way in the pages of this devotional.

Within these pages, you will find varying names to refer to God. These include Almighty, One, Creator, Divine, Elohim, El Shaddai, Jehovah, Jehovah Jireh, Lord, Most High, and Yahweh.

Questions posed in the Activities section are intended to stimulate your thought processes and guide you on the journey of relationship development with the Almighty.

Unique to each Day, the prayer is to be recited at the end of the devotion. Feel free to repeat during your day.

I pray that as you dive into the Scripture readings, connect with the reflections, ponder your responses to record in the Activities section, and say the prayers, your spiritual health will progress positively while your relationship with Yahweh is strengthened and deepened.

May you gain life-giving benefits from this devotional either alone in your personal space or with others in a cell or small group setting.

Blessings and happy reading!

Day #1

God Is.......

Acts 17:24-25, NRSVUE, [24] *"The God who made the world and everything in it, he who is LORD of heaven and earth, does not live in shrines made by human hands,* [25] *nor is he served by human hands, as though he needed anything since he himself gives to all mortals life and breath and all things."*

Reflection

Have you ever walked in a natural environment with someone younger than you? An evening stroll with one of your children or grandchildren? Perhaps you vividly recollect special childhood occasions spent with a trusted adult.

I find the level of curiosity abounding in a child rather fascinating to experience. The invaluable facial expressions reveal the child's amazement at watching nonhumans living in their natural environment. What a treasure to hear the squeals they release at the discovery of a grasshopper or small frog. Such a joy to watch their multiple attempts to touch brightly coloured butterflies.

When was the last time you allowed yourself to be so curious? Do you recall a recent occasion when your breath was taken away in amazement and awe at God's creation? Looking around at the vast array of nonhuman creatures who share this Earth with us, it is easy to stand and marvel at the diversity on display. There are countless colours, not to mention the varying shapes and sizes, with many textures to behold.

Nature is full of wonder.

As humans, we have an open invitation to take it all in, to be in awe of all we behold as we recognise how creative our Designer God is. Acknowledging this creativity reminds us of how worthy of our praise God is. El Shaddai is worthy of our adoration because of *who* God is - *the* One who created all that exists, both human and nonhuman.

Let us not be shy but rather break away from our inhibitions and freely exhibit to our Creator how awestruck we are!!!!!! Let us rejoice and celebrate the goodness of the Almighty!!!!

Activity

The following verses from the Holy Bible offer examples of words to describe our perceptions of God.

† God Almighty (NIV) †

Genesis 17:1, *"When Abram was ninety-nine years old, the LORD appeared to him and said, "I am God Almighty; walk before me faithfully and be blameless."*

† All-Sufficient (NIV) †

2 Corinthians 12:9, *"But he said to me, "My grace is sufficient for you, for my power is made perfect in weakness."*

† Trustworthy (NIV) †

Isaiah 26:3-4, *[3] "You will keep in perfect peace those whose minds are steadfast, because they trust in you. [4] Trust in the LORD forever, for the LORD, the LORD himself, is the Rock eternal."*

† Loving (KJV) †

1 John 4:7-8, *[7] "Beloved, let us love one another: for love is of God; everyone that loveth is born of God, and knoweth God. [8] He that loveth not knoweth not God; for God is love."*

There are a myriad of words one can use to describe the Almighty.

As you seek to strengthen your relationship with God, identify words or phrases that you feel most appropriately describe who God is to you.

Write these words down.

_____

_____

_____

Locate the books, chapters, and verses in the Bible that correspond with your descriptions:

_____

_____

_____

Prayer

Elohim, Creator God, you alone are worthy of praise. I magnify your name. Create in me a desire to seek after you. Abide in me, Great Jehovah. Guide me along this exciting journey of getting to know you more as I deepen and strengthen my relationship with you. Amen.

Day #2

Transformative Time Together

Mark 1:35-37, NIV, [35] *"Very early in the morning, while it was still dark, Jesus got up, left the house and went off to a solitary place, where he prayed.* [36] *Simon and his companions went to look for him,* [37] *and when they found Him, they exclaimed: "Everyone is looking for you!"*

Reflection

There are multiple places in the Bible where we read of God intentionally spending time and engaging in conversations with humankind. There is a direct discussion between Adam and Eve in the Garden of Eden (Gen. 3). God calls Moses to leadership during a conversation involving a burning bush (Exod. 3). The Book of Job narrates the lively exchanges between Job, his friends, and the questions Job's friends present before God.

Divine in human form, Jesus spoke to countless humans, including those marginalised by society. Luke 8:42-48 records Jesus, amidst a thick crowd, intentionally pausing to recognise the woman whose faith healed her of a twelve-year health challenge.

These few recollections of human interactions with the Almighty are by no means exhaustive.

I wish to draw upon two specific narratives in Genesis for your contemplation. First, after all creatures came into being in Genesis Two, God invites Adam to name each. Such an act is akin to a parent wanting to intentionally include one's child in current events. I can only surmise that this naming event was not a short process; thus, the two spent some meaningful time together. I see this as a special bonding moment and an excellent example of God seeking to be in a relationship with humankind - the created being.

Second, Jacob's prayer in Genesis 32:9-12 expressed knowledge of God as *the* God of the patriarchs and the One instructing Jacob to return to his home. The prayer reveals Jacob's fears while reiterating God's previously proclaimed promising Word. In verse 24 (NIV), we read, *"So Jacob was left alone, and a man wrestled with him till daybreak."* Jacob is without human companionship, having sent his entourage to reunite with Esau after years of separation.

The interaction occurred in the darkness of night when humans cease from hectic daytime schedules and are most likely in solitude. The night is often a time without much distraction, allowing one to focus on what is at hand.[1] I think it is fair to extrapolate that the nighttime physical struggle was not the only struggle Jacob undertook. One can attempt to envision the internal conflict Jacob

9

encountered when reflecting on past actions against others, including Esau.

Engaging in such reflections can bring about new understandings of oneself and an openness to recognising the need to remain humble in such a time of transformation.

During their time together, Jacob recognises Yahweh. Such recognition extends beyond the forefathers' faith to a *personal* understanding of who Yahweh is. Forever changed, Jacob's request to receive a mighty blessing is granted! I believe we have unlimited access to our Creator, who is willing and able to join us in discussion. I entreat you to spend quality time in God's presence so that you may be transformed!

REFERENCE

[1] "5 Important Lessons from Jacob Wrestling with God", Melanie Campbell

Retrieved from: https://www.biblestudytools.com/bible-study/topical-studies/important-lessons-from-jacobs-wrestling-match-with-god.html

Activity

Make a detailed list of your daily activities. Write down the estimated time spent on each task.

_____

_____

_____

What adjustments can be made to ensure you try to carve out special time in the day to interact with God?

_____

_____

_____

Prayer

Compassionate God, forgive me when I do not prioritise spending time with you. Forgive me when I do not converse freely with you. Awaken my senses to recognise you. Create a hunger in me for you so that I may look forward to our transformative moments together. Amen.

Day #3

Tear Up The Old and Usher In The New

Matthew 27:50 - 52, NIV, [50] *"And when Jesus had cried out again in a loud voice, he gave up his spirit.* [51] *At that moment the curtain of the temple was torn in two from top to bottom. The earth shook, the rocks split* [52] *and the tombs broke open. The bodies of many holy people who had died were raised to life."*

Reflection

Potential abounds in our ability to choose. We choose when and what to eat. We select a particular style of clothes to wear. Much time and attention is dedicated to identifying the format in which our presence will appear on social media. The list of daily decisions is never-ending.

I equate choice to freedom. It is liberation from confinement. Deciding to faithfully follow the One we acknowledge as our personal Lord and Saviour is a life-altering choice!

A vital purpose of the Tabernacle in the Old Testament was to be a holding space for the Ark of the Covenant - the indwelling place of God. Yahweh provided specific instructions for its construction.

Curtains were an important component as they partitioned the Most Holy Place from other aspects of the Tabernacle. Exquisitely embroidered with scarlet, purple, and blue yarn, these curtains symbolised the vast divide between humankind and God (Exod. 26:31,33). Once a year, the High Priest alone was permitted to pass through a specific curtain to offer sacrifices (Lev. 16:32-34).

Tearing the curtain from top to bottom (Matt. 27:50-52) indicates our Almighty's ability to do what humankind is incapable of. Divine Jesus Christ became one of us so that we who believe may receive salvation and unimpeded access to God.

Acceptance of this Truth is a choice. The sacrificial death of Jesus Christ and subsequent ripping of the curtain demonstrates the new access to our Lord (Heb. 9:11-15). Such everyday access is granted to all who choose to believe!!!

On any given day, we are bombarded with a plethora of information. We deliberately choose what information to view, share, and interact with. Negative and violent material is easily accessible in the world today.

Continually exposing ourselves to this type of material pulls our attention away from the One who created us. I ask the question - are you choosing to focus on what is life-giving? Are you deliberately choosing music, podcasts, and videos that are faith-based?

The Bible does not promise an easy life nor a life devoid of struggle. Choosing to surround ourselves with Bible-centered, positive encouragement and reinforcement of God's love for humankind releases God's presence and strength into any situation.

We can hold fast to the hope of living a life inclusive of the Trinity - God the Almighty, God the Son, and God the Holy Spirit.

What a Blessing to have such a choice!!!

Activity

Think of your choice to accept Jesus Christ as your personal Lord and Saviour. Write down a few sentences which describe the impact such a decision has had on your life.

_____

_____

_____

What does having direct access to God mean for your life?

_____

_____

_____

If you have not accepted Jesus Christ as your personal Lord and Saviour, what are the main reasons for not doing so?

_____

_____

_____

What everyday obstacles hinder your desire to spend time with your Creator?

_____

_____

_____

Prayer

Loving God, you have shown me how much you love me by removing the veil, a symbol of separation between you and me. Today and every day, may I focus on the gift of direct access to you. Forgive me if I take this offered access for granted. Be with me in my humble quest to be in your presence each and every day. Amen.

Day #4

Boldly I Ask, Humbly I Hear

John 4:5-14, NIV, [5] *"So he came to a town in Samaria called Sychar, near the plot of ground Jacob had given to his son Joseph.* [6] *Jacob's well was there, and Jesus, tired as he was from the journey, sat down by the well. It was about noon.*

[7] *When a Samaritan woman came to draw water, Jesus said to her, "Will you give me a drink?"* [8] *(His disciples had gone into the town to buy food.)*

[9] *The Samaritan woman said to him, "You are a Jew and I am a Samaritan woman. How can you ask me for a drink?" (For Jews do not associate with Samaritans.)* [10] *Jesus answered her, "If you knew the gift of God and who it is that asks you for a drink, you would have asked him, and he would have given you living water."*

[11] *"Sir," the woman said, "you have nothing to draw with, and the well is deep. Where can you get this living water?* [12] *Are you greater than our father Jacob, who gave us the well and drank from it, as did his sons and his livestock?"*

> [13] Jesus answered, "Everyone who drinks this water will be thirsty again, [14] but whoever drinks the water I give them will never thirst. Indeed, the water I give them will become in them a spring of water welling up to eternal life."

Reflection

The dialogue between the 'Woman at the Well' and Jesus leaves us with significant and lasting impressions. This woman is quite astute and intelligent, with a keen ability to quickly comprehend.

Her initial statement promptly points the reader to the reality of the day - a time when Jews did not associate with Samaritans. Despite the social divide, she does not appear shy with this friendly stranger who willingly converses with her. During her exchange with Jesus Christ, the unnamed woman is not afraid to boldly ask a few questions.

We recognise her desire to pursue Truth throughout the frank and open discussion. Unashamedly, she continuously searches for clarity through her series of questions. She wisely discerns that should she have the living water Christ speaks of, her life will forever be transformed.

Her perseverance is rewarded as Christ reveals His Truth!! Jesus seized the opportune moment to reveal Himself to her, to make the pronouncement. John 4:26, NRSVUE, *"Jesus said to her, "I am he, the one who is speaking to you."*

This Scripture reinforces how powerfully intimate, one-on-one chats with the All-Sufficient God are. Hope is given to those who feel shunned, unloved, and judged by others. As revelations spring forth and new insights surface, our awareness of the Truth is heightened. Rejuvenation and reinvigoration can now occur in our minds and thought processes when we freely raise questions to the Most High.

Asking questions of One so Divine opened the door for this woman to pay it forward by revealing truths to her fellow townsfolk. Her testimony, in John 4:39-42, caused others to believe that Jesus was, in fact, *the* Messiah. Being willing and open to spending time alone with the Divine while eagerly embracing the revelations received allows us to become conduits of good—sufficient and powerful enough to extend that goodness to others!

Activity

Matthew 7:7-11 extends an invitation to freely and openly speak with God. Through dialogue, clarity can be attained. Take a moment to read this Scripture.

Identify a few verses in The Bible that are confusing and unclear.

Make a list of them.

_____

_____

_____

_____

_____

Ask God to provide you with a greater understanding as you read over these Scriptures.

_____

_____

_____

Prayer

Thank you, Great Jehovah, for loving me right where I am. How considerate of you to accept me with my imperfections. As I strive to explore more about your Truth, may I be neither timid nor shy but boldly present my questions before You. Bless me with the ability to clearly discern your responses. Amen.

Day #5

Daily Shall I Do

Deuteronomy 6:4-9, NIV, [4]*"Hear, O Israel: The LORD our God, the LORD is one.* [5]*Love the LORD your God with all your heart and with all your soul and with all your strength.* [6]*These commandments that I give you today are to be on your hearts.* [7]*Impress them on your children. Talk about them when you sit at home and when you walk along the road, when you lie down and when you get up.* [8]*Tie them as symbols on your hands and bind them on your foreheads.* [9]*Write them on the doorframes of your houses and on your gates."*

Reflection

My mornings are very hectic, as I try to leave the house on time. Ideally, my bag(s) would be packed the previous night and sitting circumspectly by the front door, waiting to be collected on my way out. My reality is somewhat different. As I race about the house getting ready, my mind thinks of the day ahead. I envision those items I need and attempt to gather and pack them before I leave through the front door, holding my handbag and lunch bag.

During my early morning movements, I would use or charge my phone and drink from the water bottle. When my mind is preoccupied, I will set them down anywhere. If in a hurry, retrieving the items before I exit is sometimes a neglected step. On occasion, as I was driving to my destination, I noticed that my cell phone or water bottle was not with me. A decision to turn around to retrieve either object means the journey to my destination has to begin all over again.

Admittedly, my regular routine presents a challenge; therefore, I need to make adjustments to ensure I don't forget essential items. I know how quickly and easily I forget when in a rush. I choose to make a concerted effort to pre-pack my bags.

If I cannot pack my bags the night before, I now take extra steps to do so in the morning. I try to look at the items I place in the vehicle and ensure everything is present. The few extra minutes of this purposeful act saves me time in the long run while eliminating the frustration of turning around. I want to intentionally do what I feel is required to eliminate wasting energy and time.

I continue to be a work in progress.

God shares wise advice with the Israelites living outside Egypt in Deuteronomy 6. They are living a new life. With the granted freedom came many changes. Intentionally focusing on imprinting God's Word on their hearts is a powerful way to guide them through the ordeals they would experience. This Scripture reminds me of how vital it is to walk daily with God's Word deep within my heart.

In this era of busyness and forgetfulness, I choose to remember the goodness of Elohim by deliberately spending quality time in Holy Scripture, which is a life-giving and necessary companion along this journey called Life.

Activity

Take a moment to find a quiet space. Perhaps it is a special place in your home or your garden. If possible, walk on a favourite nature trail or in a park.

As you walk, listen to the audio version of Psalm 34.

_____

_____

_____

Make notes - what are you grateful for at this moment?

_____

_____

_____

Prayer

Glorious Saviour, I am grateful you are a patient God. Sometimes, I move about too quickly to attain worldly gains. Forgive me for being caught up in the busyness of life. Forgive me for not carving out special and specific time to spend with you. Cultivate in me the seed of intentionality so that I may daily recognise your mercies, both great and small. Amen.

Day #6

I Will Empty My Cup
So I Can Be Set Free!!

---

1 Samuel 1:12-17, NIV, *12 "As she kept on praying to the LORD, Eli observed her mouth. 13 Hannah was praying in her heart, and her lips were moving but her voice was not heard. Eli thought she was drunk 14 and said to her, "How long are you going to stay drunk? Put away your wine."*

15 "Not so, my lord," Hannah replied, "I am a woman who is deeply troubled. I have not been drinking wine or beer; I was pouring out my soul to the LORD. 16 Do not take your servant for a wicked woman; I have been praying here out of my great anguish and grief."

17 Eli answered, "Go in peace, and may the God of Israel grant you what you have asked of him."

Reflection

I have grown to appreciate communication as having many forms. It is not verbal alone. Non-verbal communication is an extremely powerful tool. In those moments when I am in emotional pain, experiencing a particularly difficult situation, or processing something terrible that has happened to a loved one, I know it is time to lay prostrate on the floor and bare my soul in the best way possible. As I continue to strengthen and deepen my relationship with God, I know with certainty that Jehovah Jireh <u>will</u> provide a listening ear to me and all who request a presence.

When I received the calling to further my education at the tertiary level, it had been many years since I last held instructional academic books. I was physically separated from family, familiar people, and places. During those years, I gained a deeper understanding of the width and depth of Divine calling. Receiving a call does not mean the response road will be easy or smooth.

Reading and completing the mandatory assignments was challenging at times. There were moments when it became overwhelming, and I was deeply troubled. I could not see how I would get through it all. Within those academic years, there were two or three instances where it was necessary to release pent-up emotions. I would cease what I was doing, step away from my work table, and lay on the ground.

Releasing what was cooped up inside both audibly and inaudibly was refreshing. Knowing God is always accessible, willing, and ready to hear me was comforting. I sought solace in my private space, crying out to the Almighty.

In 1 Samuel 1, verse 10, NIV, we read that Hannah is in "...*deep anguish*" and "... *weeping bitterly.*" Peninnah, Elkanah's other wife, tormented Hannah because of her barrenness, and it is now evident such provocation had pushed Hannah to a breaking point. Pent-up emotions needed to be released. At the Temple, Hannah spoke prayers, verse 13, "...*in her heart*," confident her Creator could hear and fully comprehend her torment and sorrow.

She broke down in a prime location - the Temple of the Lord. The ultimate location to lay bare all to the One who cares. The One who is always welcoming and willing to hear our petitions.

We, too, can be confident that handing it all over to the Almighty is wise when we are hurting and in deep anguish. Rest assured - God hears and truly understands the depth of our internal pain. Wherever we are - in our homes, at work, or in our vehicles - we have direct access to our Loving God.

Reference

"1 Samuel 1: The Birth of Samuel". David Guzik's Bible Commentary.

Retrieved from: https://enduringword.com/bible-commentary/1-samuel-1/

Activity

Is there a situation or challenge that has touched you deeply? Write down the issue(s).

_____

_____

_____

Just as Hannah poured out her heart to the Lord in the Temple, in words or sounds incomprehensible to human ears, take time to unashamedly bare your soul.

_____

_____

_____

Prayer

Be the center of my life, oh Lord, as I seek to live a life pleasing in your sight. I confess that I fall short in so many ways. I often wait until a challenge arises before I open up to you. Help me learn to communicate with you in the good and not-so-good moments. Amen.

Day #7

Jehovah Jireh:

The Lord Will Provide

1 Kings 17:6, NIV, "The ravens brought him bread and meat in the morning and bread and meat in the evening, and he drank from the brook."

Psalm 23:1-3, NIV, [1] "The LORD is my shepherd, I lack nothing. [2] He makes me lie down in green pastures, he leads me beside quiet waters, [3] he refreshes my soul. He guides me along the right paths for his name's sake."

Reflection

Mummy would spend hours in her garden. She held a deep appreciation for nature and the creatures of the Earth. Growing up, wild pigeons frequented our yard in search of food. Although she had never learned to drive, Mummy ensured feed was purchased routinely for their nourishment. They came like clockwork every single morning. Even after all these years, I can vividly recall the intense flapping of wings and loud cooing noises as they tried to outdo each other to gain access to the bird feed.

Birds are featured throughout the Bible. God instructs the Israelites to use birds as sacrificial offerings in Leviticus 15:14. The strength of Eagles is referenced in Psalm 103:5 and Isaiah 40:31.

First Kings chronicles the ministry of Elijah, the prophet, Yahweh's mouthpiece, and one of two prophets who visits Jesus on the Mount of Transfiguration. Elijah was aware of the impending drought over the land when God instructed him to deliver the news to the King. Elijah had no need to fear the imminent event as God had a detailed plan for Elijah's protection. One that entailed leaving where he was and traveling to new places.

Elijah obediently went where God directed him, fully trusting that he would be cared for. The depth of Elijah's relationship with Yahweh is evident in the meticulous manner in which Yahweh ensures his survival during that period of drought. Birds, specifically ravens, are the medium by which nourishment and refreshment are provided to the Prophet.

Israel's drought lasted for over three years, according to 1 Kings 18:1. For those three years, ravens obediently provided food in the morning and evening. There is no mention of lack.

I have experienced dry seasons, periods of feeling emotionally or spiritually empty and drained. They are painful seasons. A lot of energy is consumed focusing on attempting to get through the day. My intentional acts of reading the Bible, attending worship services, and spending time alone with the Almighty keep me going. I hold fast to my hope and knowledge that God truly cares for me and desires for me to enjoy my life.

I encourage you to do the same. Pray. Read the Bible version of your choice. Sit and be still in God's presence. Whether in a season of drought or joy, rest in the assurance that our Yahweh can and will provide more than is sufficient to get us through. Trust Him, realising our provision may not be in our anticipated format. God knows our needs and can meet and exceed them at the most appropriate time.

Reference

"Who Was Elijah in the Bible?" David Sanford, Feb. 21 Updated Sept. 13, 2023. Retrieved from: https://www.christianity.com/wiki/people/who-was-elijah-in-the-bible.html

Activity

The animal kingdom is vast. Take a moment to think about which animals you admire. Describe specific traits you find most interesting about the animal.

_____

_____

_____

If you cannot consider an animal, respond with feedback on a member of the plant kingdom.

_____

_____

_____

Prayer

Majestic One, your creativity knows no limits. You have interconnected humans and nonhumans in this world to fulfill your will. May I be wise enough to know how to protect and conserve this Earth for the future of humankind and non-humankind. Thank you for always being near enough to hear me. Thank you for always knowing when I need to be refreshed and recharged. Amen.

Day #8

Seek Out The Wisdom You Need

Reflection

On any given Sunday, you would have found Mummy and I in the front room with the door swung wide open. Alarms were being raised about global warming then. Still, the weather was bearable for our homes without air conditioners. It was customary for me to pray for some breeze to meander through.

I can fully appreciate those Sunday afternoons as I know how precious such occasions were. It was my time to glean as much as possible as I sat at the matriarch's feet. Her enlightening conversations were my history lessons. History revealed through her eyes was so enriching. Mummy spoke to a time before we gained Independence from Great Britain. A time when the currency was not Bahamian dollars and cents but British pounds and pence. A time when the dominant mode of transportation was horse-drawn carriages.

I heard stories about her life. The hardships and lessons learned. She chose to share with me much like the author of Ecclesiastes shared with the student. Wise words were imparted on those easygoing Sunday afternoons. Dramatic narratives were shared as our unshakeable love was cemented.

If there was any question I wanted to ask or a situation I was struggling with, Sunday afternoon was the time to discuss it so that I may gain her wisdom and insight. With each lesson, she imparted two crucial, all-encompassing pieces of wisdom. I need to remember to worship and honour our Creator God. Life is difficult and requires work; however, one can make it through with faith in the Almighty.

Our opening scripture from Proverbs encourages us to search for knowledge. James states that we should all seek God's face to attain wisdom. The journey through life is filled with countless challenges, twists, turns, and situations that require thoughtful ways of addressing them.

Hear me when I say difficult situations will arise despite our best efforts. Yet, as one who believes in the Divine, I hold on to hope. I gain relief and comfort knowing I do not have to traverse this life alone. I know I can gain much from reading the Holy Bible, which is replete with God's direction, advice, guidance, and wisdom on how to live daily.

I invite you to also seek knowledge by deepening your relationship with the All-Wise God. Pursuing wisdom and insight will require new ways of thinking and doing. Mummy taught me not to rely on myself but to willingly learn how to lean on God. She encouraged me to align myself with other believers, and I also suggest gathering with others whose beliefs are similar to yours to experience a more fulfilling life.

Activity

Have you had an opportunity to sit with an elderly family member? Now may be the best time to call and chat with them. Write down a few questions you would ask.

_____

_____

_____

Are there any other topics you seek to learn more about? Jot them down.

_____

_____

_____

If you can, visit a Senior citizen's home or the local hospital and spend time with an elderly person. There is a wealth of knowledge and history from which you can glean when you do.

Prayer

Thank you, Wise God, for the gifts of discernment and wisdom. I am at peace knowing I do not have to endure each day alone. Bless me with the guidance and knowledge only you can provide. Renew in me the ability to discern your anointing on my life so that I may live to the fullest and enjoy all the Blessings you have set aside for me! Amen.

$\mathcal{D}ay$ #9

Safe In The Arms

of The Almighty

Isaiah 43:1-3, NIV[1] But now, this is what the LORD says— he who created you, Jacob, who formed you, Israel: "Do not fear, for I have redeemed you; I have summoned you by name; you are mine. [2] When you pass through the waters, I will be with you; when you pass through the rivers, they will not sweep over you. When you walk through the fire, you will not be burned; the flames will not set you ablaze. [3] For I am the LORD your God, the Holy One of Israel, your Savior..."

Reflection

Many of us have utilised air travel for some reason during our lifetime - for work, pleasure, or to visit family members or loved ones living far away. Major travel options for those who live on an island include sea or air transport. Growing up, traveling by airplane was my preferred means of transport.

I am sure many of you know the ins and outs of traveling. Arriving at the airport for some form of check-in or luggage drop-off before trudging through airport security lines before boarding the flight. Whatever your assigned seat is, aisle, middle, or window, once the door is shut, no one can move about freely for a prolonged period. If you are like me, you have said many prayers during take-off, landing, and during the flight.

One specific memory stands out in my mind as unforgettable. On an overnight flight across the Atlantic Ocean, all was well for the first few hours. I was settling in comfortably and about to close my eyes for a nap when we hit turbulent weather. Surrounded by darkness, the plane moved erratically from side to side. It felt like the pilot was maneuvering a vehicle at high speed on an interstate highway.

The feeling of complete helplessness took over me. At that moment, I had absolutely *no* control over the situation. All on board were at the mercy of those flying the airplane. While weaving from side to side, I repeatedly recited the Lord's Prayer. I may have had no physical control, but I held, and continue to hold, fast to my belief in the power of prayer! As the pilot flew the plane, I had confidence the Divine was in control.

Isaiah 43 reminds us that life is not without scary situations. There will be moments in which we will feel completely exposed and unable to gain control of what is going on around us. In those instances, we are to remember God's promise that we are not alone, are fully protected, and will not be harmed. As scary as the current calamity is, rest assured that you are cared for and loved. Find peace in the assurance that Our Creator claims you and me as one who belongs in the safe company of the Almighty!!

Activity

Reflect on your life to date. Which life storms or difficult times stand out in your memory? Write them down if you are able.

_____

_____

_____

What emotions were felt when you were in the most challenging part of the storm?

_____

_____

_____

Record the Blessings you experienced amid the storms.

_____

_____

_____

Prayer

Almighty God, you knew me before I knew myself. Again and again, I can attest to your protecting me from harm. Keep me under the shelter of your loving, outstretched arms. Allow your protection to rain down on me and my loved ones now and forevermore. Amen.

Day #10

Together

John 6:5-11, NIV, [5] *"When Jesus looked up and saw a great crowd coming toward him, he said to Philip, "Where shall we buy bread for these people to eat?"* [6] *He asked this only to test him, for he already had in mind what he was going to do.* [7] *Philip answered him, "It would take more than half a year's wages to buy enough bread for each one to have a bite!"* [8] *Another of his disciples, Andrew, Simon Peter's brother, spoke up,* [9] *"Here is a boy with five small barley loaves and two small fish, but how far will they go among so many?"* [10] *Jesus said, "Have the people sit down." There was plenty of grass in that place, and they sat down (about five thousand men were there).* [11] *Jesus then took the loaves, gave thanks, and distributed to those who were seated as much as they wanted. He did the same with the fish."*

Reflection

The Messiah invited twelve disciples to walk alongside Him as He engaged in ministry. Inviting each disciple into the group demonstrated an intentional and specific act. One can only imagine the emotions felt after being granted entry into the inner circle, the undocumented life-altering events, and the inner workings they were exposed to. By being members of this group, the disciples are willingly (or unwillingly) connected.

Jesus performed countless miracles. Wherever He went, large crowds were drawn towards Him. Many were eager to witness for themselves the many wonders He performed. Our association with others, intentional or unintentional, places us in a community. We are connected within our homes, our places of worship, on the job site, and in any area where others coexist. We are in a relationship of some form.

By God's grace, these connections will yield positive results. Being in a relationship with the Triune God yields healthy results. It is important to note that such results are derived over time and constant interaction. Results come when you are willing and open to change. If you desire to yield to that which is greater than you are - I implore you to know and believe in your heart that with our Triune God, *anything* is possible.

In John 6:5-11, we recognise that although Jesus' plan was already formatted, Jesus offered Philip the opportunity to participate. Philip was not ready to seize the opportunity. It is Andrew who readily provides a suggestion. Why not utilise the boy's humble meal?

It is unexpected, impossible even, for the boy's modest meal to be able to feed so many. Yet, Andrew rose to the occasion of agreeing with Jesus' <u>ability</u> to feed and provide for the large community.

Such an undertaking was impossible for a mere human, but Jesus, Jesus can perform miracles!!

Fellow believers, there are many social settings in which we can interact with others. Don't be afraid to make connections. Allow yourself to be a part of something greater than you can ever imagine. Be ready to witness firsthand what is humanly impossible. Our All-Sufficient Lord can connect you with others desiring such partnerships so that you can be used in wondrous ways as you Bless others in your community!!!

Activity

What communities are you intentionally and unintentionally a member of?

_____

_____

_____

Think of those occasions when God moved unexpectedly in one of those communities.

_____

_____

_____

What direct impact did such a move have on the community?

_____

_____

_____

Were you directly involved? If so, what was your role? If not, how were you impacted?

_____

_____

_____

Prayer

Gracious and loving God, forgive me when I forget how awesome you are. When I doubt or neglect to remember your wondrous ways, create in me a curiosity to discover you again and again. May I not shy away from opportunities to witness to others so that we may build up your Kingdom together. Amen.

Day #11

Complete Surrender

1 *Samuel 15:22-23, NIV,* [22] *"But Samuel replied: "Does the LORD delight in burnt offerings and sacrifices as much as in obeying the LORD? To obey is better than sacrifice, and to heed is better than the fat of rams.* [23] *For rebellion is like the sin of divination, and arrogance like the evil of idolatry. Because you have rejected the Word of the LORD, he has rejected you as King."*

Reflection

Often, we do not recognise the value of someone until that person is no longer in our lives. What a pleasure it was to live with my grandaunt, a wise sage and an able historian. Both comical and caring, Mummy was my first storyteller. Many within our community sought out her wise counsel.

Our relationship was not without its occasional static, but I held my mother in high regard and deeply appreciated her opening up her heart and home to me. Mummy frequently recited numerous phrases, one of which was, "Obedience is better than sacrifice...." For many years, I considered this phrase confusing.

In my view, obedience frequently demands sacrifice in some shape or form. "Obedience is better than sacrifice...." I have wrestled with these words for decades. As time has passed, my desire to dig deeper into and understand the Word of God has increased. I have gained a greater understanding as I mature into my faith (not of others as in my early faith) and continue to read and reread Holy Scripture for myself.

There is so much more to uncover. In the spiritual realm, the heart is essential. In the Book of Jeremiah, chapter 17, we read that the heart is difficult to understand. Proverbs chapter 4 instructs us to guard our hearts as it is a reservoir from which a spring freely flows.

I am now able to appreciate how powerful the heart is. It cultivates and creates. Out of the heart springs one's desires, wants, and motives. Deep within the body, the heart and its contents are invisible to the human eye yet fully exposed to the all-seeing eyes of our Lord. God seeks those whose hearts are not devoted to pleasuring themself but rather entirely focused on Divine will and that alone. It requires a total and complete surrendering of oneself.

To crave a relationship with our Creator equates to a strong desire to do that which is pleasing to the One Triune God. Our heart then longs to do what is right in the sight of the Almighty. The heart seeks to feed on the Word of God. Nourishing oneself with the Word progresses naturally to surrendering to the will of the

Almighty. In doing so, the mind will not be allowed to fester on thoughts that oppose the Almighty's will.

Yes, sacrifice often accompanies obedience when we yearn to walk with God. However, when we aspire to obey God's will and be obedient, the corresponding sacrifice is not a burden; it is both an honour and a blessing!!!

Activity

Reflect upon varying periods in your life. Make notes about when you obediently followed and adhered to a Word God shared with you.

_____

_____

_____

Were there occasions when you received instructions from God and, for some reason, you did not live out or follow the instructions? Write a few sentences about such occasions.

_____

_____

_____

Describe the emotions experienced when you submitted to the Word of God and did not.

_____

_____

_____

Prayer

Compassionate Saviour, your name is above every name. I am nothing without you. Search my heart. Remove any darkness, any substance that is not aligned with you, and replace it with a yearning to know and do your will more and more each day. Amen.

Day #12

God's Outstretched Arm
and Mighty Hand

Matthew 14:25-33, NIV, *[25] "Shortly before dawn Jesus went out to them, walking on the lake. [26] When the disciples saw him walking on the lake, they were terrified. "It's a ghost," they said, and cried out in fear.*

[27] But Jesus immediately said to them: "Take courage! It is I. Don't be afraid."

[28] "Lord, if it's you," Peter replied, "tell me to come to you on the water."

[29] "Come," he said.

Then Peter got down out of the boat, walked on the water and came toward Jesus. [30] But when he saw the wind, he was afraid and, beginning to sink, cried out, "Lord, save me!"

31 Immediately Jesus reached out his hand and caught him. "You of little faith," he said, "why did you doubt?" 32 And when they climbed into the boat, the wind died down. 33 Then those who were in the boat worshiped him, saying, "Truly you are the Son of God."

Reflection

Have you ever listened to Senior Citizens, anyone over sixty, greet one another? When in earshot of two Elders, I've usually found the opening exchanges attention-grabbing and occasionally amusing. One phrase, usually exchanged between women, stands out in my mind. A lone response to an inquiry as to how the other was keeping. "Right here between oh Lord and thank God!"

Hmmmm.... what do they mean by that? As I mull over that expression in my mind, I have come to a conclusion. Each breath should be used to praise God and to give thanks for all the Merciful Lord is doing. There are those moments, however, when things look rough, and there is a need to shout, "Oh Lord, I need thee!"

Our Opening Scripture reading is nestled within a chapter replete with activity. The gruesome death of John the Baptist, the forerunner of Jesus Christ, at the hands of the King opens the chapter before quickly moving on to the miracle feeding of the five thousand. Afterward, the disciples are sent away in a boat, leaving Christ alone in prayer. As dawn approaches, Christ joins the disciples by walking on the water.

The early morning light has not risen yet, and understandably, the disciples are afraid of the sight before their eyes. Peter overcomes his fear and steps out of the boat. Yet, like many of us, his initial bravery quickly turned to apprehension when he saw what was happening around him. Ever near when we call, Jesus did not hesitate. Our Redeemer reached out to extend His hand the *instant* Peter cried out.

That's what I call an immediate response!!!

What peace is extended to us as we traverse through perilous times. The Triune God is *always* available to us. May we remain assured that everything is not lost. Let us have faith in what God is capable of and trust that we are protected and cared for. Regardless of how the winds of life blow, may we each depend upon the Almighty to respond when we call or feel like we are sinking into deep waters. Rest assured, just as Jesus reacted immediately to Peter's cry for help, Jehovah Jireh will do the same for you!!

Activity

Reflect upon a specific time when you heard God encouraging you to do something new - to move forward with boldness!!

_____

_____

_____

Perhaps you were being told to accept the new position offer or open a business. Record what you were told.

_____

_____

_____

Did the nudge cause you to move forward? Why or why not?

_____

_____

_____

Reflect upon a time you made a bold move. Do you feel you were more afraid or more adventurous? What would you have done differently?

_____

_____

_____

Think about your life to date. Write down specific moments you realised God's favour was upon you, especially during difficult times.

_____

_____

_____

Prayer

Merciful God, thank you for the peace of knowing you are ever present, even amid life's storms. When the strong winds rage around me, when I am afraid of present situations, thank you for the comfort of holding on to your outstretched arm and unwavering hand. Amen.

Day #13

My Faith Will Set Me Free

Mark 5:24–34, NIV, [24] *"A large crowd followed and pressed around him.* [25] *And a woman was there who had been subject to bleeding for twelve years.* [26] *She had suffered a great deal under the care of many doctors and had spent all she had, yet instead of getting better, she grew worse.* [27] *When she heard about Jesus, she came up behind him in the crowd and touched his cloak* [28] *because she thought, "If I just touch his clothes, I will be healed."* [29] *Immediately, her bleeding stopped, and she felt in her body that she was freed from her suffering.* [30] *At once, Jesus realized that power had gone out from him. He turned around in the crowd and asked, "Who touched my clothes?"* [31] *"You see the people crowding against you," his disciples answered, "and yet you can ask, 'Who touched me?'"* [32] *But Jesus kept looking around to see who had done it.* [33] *Then the woman, knowing what had happened to her, came and fell at his feet and, trembling with fear, told him the whole truth.* [34] *He told her, "Daughter, your faith has healed you. Go in peace and be freed from your suffering."*

Reflection

History tells of a societal practice of the day that shunned the sick (Lev. 13; Luke 17). I could not fathom the discomfort this unnamed woman had experienced, both physically and socially. Additionally, she faced a harsh reality of exclusion when forced to live on the outskirts of society. It is difficult to imagine an ever-present existence of invisibility.

The Gospel of Mark notes the unnamed woman has lived with the disorder for twelve years, yet we see no record of this woman choosing to sit still or wallow in self-pity. Rather than bemoan her situation, she faces it head-on by pursuing treatment after treatment at the hands of many medical doctors who had reportedly drained her finances with no positive results.

Despite her harsh health circumstances, feelings of discomfort, and financial distress, she refused to give up. The world told her she was unwelcomed, unseen, and without a voice. Yet,this woman's willpower remained strong and resolute in the hope that the Almighty's grace would be poured out on her.

One can surmise that hearing the stories of Christ's miracles led her to create a simple plan - get close enough for a mere touch! Throngs of people eager to see and be around Christ did not deter her steadfastness. She knew one touch and her life would forever be changed!

I pray you agree with me when I say what an inspiration this unnamed woman is! Her story is one of both encouragement and motivation. The actions of this nameless woman demonstrate determination and persistence. She opposes acceptable societal norms and holds fast to faith in Divine grace.

Her faith motivated her to continue despite the many failed attempts at long-lasting peace. The Messiah intentionally pauses to search for the one who has sought Him out. Unaccustomed to being the center of attention, her reverence for Jesus shines through as she speaks her Truth.

No deception nor casting blame on others; confession takes center stage as her story is openly shared among strangers. A shift occurs. Her invisibility and lack of a social identity fell away when Jesus referred to her as "daughter." May we be as bold and determined in our faith as this unnamed woman and receive the Blessings of Peace and Freedom only the Divine can provide.

Activity

Describe those seasons of your life when you felt invisible and unnoticed by others.

_____

_____

_____

How long did those seasons last? What did you do during that time?

_____

_____

_____

In this present moment, are you motivated to reach out to God for something specific?

_____

_____

_____

What is it that you desire to receive? What are you seeking from God? Be descriptive.

_____

_____

_____

Prayer

Gracious God, sometimes I turn to others pursuing answers when I should bring my challenges to you. I pray that I may emulate the positive qualities of this Unnamed Woman. May I be as determined, courageous, and unafraid to come before thee as she was. Thank you for receiving me as I bare my soul to you, my Lord and Saviour. Amen.

Day #14

Honouring God In My Profession

Exodus 1:8-10, and 1:15-17, NIV, *[8:] "Then a new king, to whom Joseph meant nothing, came to power in Egypt. [9] "Look," he said to his people, "the Israelites have become far too numerous for us. [10] Come, we must deal shrewdly with them, or they will become even more numerous and...*

[15] The King of Egypt said to the Hebrew midwives, whose names were Shiphrah and Puah, [16] "When you are helping the Hebrew women during childbirth on the delivery stool, if you see that the baby is a boy, kill him; but if it is a girl, let her live." [17] The midwives, however, feared God and did not do what the King of Egypt had told them to do; they let the boys live."

Reflection

This devotional has insufficient room to discuss the depth of history and wisdom within the pages of the Book of Exodus. Its contents are fascinating to read, from the description of the burning bush to the revelation of who *Elohim* is, Exod. 3:14, NIV, *"God said to Moses, "I AM WHO I AM"* announced before the commissioning of a hesitant and stuttering Moses. The story of the parting of the Red Sea after the freeing of a bonded and oppressed people is both awe-striking and hope-inspiring for all believers.

My focus for this devotional lies within the opening lines of chapter one, where we read about the multiplication of the Israelites in the land of Egypt. A land that currently held no regard for God nor all that had been accomplished by Jacob's son Joseph. History is now at a crossroads where the notions of creation, provision, and multiplication are at stake.

Pharoah's directive to the midwives in verse 16 directly contrasts God's plan for creation. Regardless of the authority Pharoah held, it paled in comparison to the authority of our Creator. Because of their reverence for the Almighty, they sought to please the Creator and not some imposter. Already serving in a ministry that witnessed the welcoming of miraculous new life into the world, the midwives refused to allow an anti-creational plan to prevail. They were non-compliant with Pharoah's order to kill Israelite baby boys.

These midwives exuded bravery. They chose to partner with our Creator God and stood against the plan of the adversary to wipe out the Israelites. The actions of the midwives should be applauded. We can learn lessons from their willingness to serve God amid a difficult situation. The midwives worked diligently. They do not appear to be self-serving nor craving praise from others. They remained faithful to their profession, a ministry in and of itself.

Yahweh was cognizant of their efforts and provided a reward for their bravery, Exod. 1:20, NIV, *"So God was kind to the midwives..."*. As we reflect upon this narrative within the broader Exodus story, may we also recommit ourselves to our respective professions with the highest regard for the life and health of others. May we execute our tasks daily with compassion and reverence for Our All-Knowing Maker!

Believers, may we read this as a story of hope and gain a new level of adoration for who our Maker is.

Activity

Does your current job, position, or career bring you satisfaction?

_____

_____

_____

Are there any mandated tasks that are challenging to complete?

_____

_____

_____

Do you struggle because you feel the tasks conflict with your Christian beliefs?

_____

_____

_____

In what way have you addressed such conflicts?

_____

_____

_____

Have you sought the advice of church leaders, elders, or others who can provide guidance?

_____

_____

_____

Prayer

All Knowing God, I am grateful for this example of bravery and fearlessness. Guide me to discern your plans for my professional life. Help me take my responsibilities to family, faith community, and career as seriously and with such conviction as the midwives did so that I may live a life pleasing to you. Amen.

Day #15

I Am Meant To Be Here!!!

Proverbs 20:5, NIV, [5:] *"The purposes of a person's heart are deep waters, but one who has insight draws them out."*

Psalm 57, 1-2, NRSVUE, [1] *"Be merciful to me, O God; be merciful to me, for in you my soul takes refuge; in the shadow of your wings I will take refuge until the destroying storms pass by.* [2] *I cry to God Most High, to God who fulfills his purpose for me."*

Reflection

I have two close friends who knew early on what profession they would enter as adults. One aspired to be a physician; the other an accountant. I have long admired them for their steadfastness and dedication. They studied hard in high school before obtaining degrees in their respective fields from tertiary institutions.

Ever progressive, they seized other learning opportunities, including internships, special certification courses, and advanced classes. Each is now considered to be in the top echelons of their respective professions and living out what I feel is their purpose.

In comparison, I had no idea what profession I would enter. I did not have a career path planned; thus, my professional journey has endured its share of twists and turns. I appreciate the reality that the paths I have taken in life have enabled me to see and do so much more than I could have imagined as a child. Along the way I have gathered a few stories and pleasant memories by the Lord's grace and mercy.

Reflecting on it all, I have come to a few conclusions. It is okay to take time, years even, to recognise my vocational strengths. Each of us is Blessed with unique talents and gifts. I now acknowledge that my individuality makes me who I am. The global pandemic brought to light the harsh reality that anyone's life could shift at any moment. During that period, I spent time in self-reflection and introspection.

I intentionally tried to awaken my senses to the point of identifying ways to maximise my capabilities. I invite you to ask yourself - are you finding fulfillment in what you do daily? Are you pursuing that which gives you inner joy and maintains your inner peace? More specifically, are you fulfilling your God-ordained purpose?

The motivation to attain the responses to these heavy questions points me in one direction - toward my Creator. Who else can aptly guide and direct me towards that which will bring me joy? Who better to know what I was created to do than the One who knit me together in the womb? To receive the responses, I must pause to open the doors of my spiritual senses so that communication can freely flow.

The invitation is extended to all of us in Matthew 7:7-8, NIV, *7 "Ask, and it will be given to you; seek, and you will find; knock and the door will be opened to you. 8 For everyone who asks receives; the one who seeks finds; and to the one who knocks, the door will be opened. "*

Are you curious enough to search? Can you trust, receive, accept, and live out what you discern for your life?

Activity

1. Sit in a comfortable space.
2. Set your alarm for a set time of 5, 15, or 30 minutes.
3. Say out loud your intentions for this time. Communicate your desire to know more about your purpose. Say something like, "God, I am here, willing to hear from you; help me understand how I can have a positive impact on the lives of others."
4. Be still for your chosen time. Every time your mind begins to wander, bring it back under control. Focus on the here and now.
5. Listen for God's voice.
6. Make any notes about what you heard.

_____

_____

_____

Prayer

Renew my heart with purpose, oh Lord. Fan the flames which burn deep inside me to go where you direct me to go and do as you instruct me to do with boldness, humility, and steadfastness. Remind me often that my life has meaning and purpose for me, my family, and the many others I am here to serve. Amen.

Day #16

The Bitter Taste of Sweet Fruit

(Patience)

Galatians 5:22-23, NRSVUE, [22] *"By contrast, the fruit of the Spirit is love, joy, peace, patience, kindness, generosity, faithfulness,* [23] *gentleness, and self-control."*

Reflection

The Bible is full of fascinating stories. Some of those stories are of persons who teach us the difficult lesson of patience. Within the pages of the Old and New Testaments are examples of persons receiving a promised Word or vision from God. However, the full manifestation of God's plan was not immediate.

We need only look at the opening pages of the first book of the Bible, which contains the well-known narrative of Genesis 12. God bestows the promise of nation-building upon the patriarch.

Genesis 12:4 confirms Abram (whose name was subsequently changed to Abraham) was seventy-five years old and childless. The promised heir, Isaac, is born to Abraham the centurion (100 years old) and his ninety-year-old wife Sarah (Gen. 21:5). It took approximately twenty-five years for the promised offspring to arrive and even longer for a nation to come to fruition!

Genesis also shares the narrative of Joseph. The young son of Jacob and Rebecca, whose dreams were not fully understood until more than a decade later. *After* Joseph had endured many trials and tribulations, he came to discover the depth and reach of the dreams (Gen. 50:15-20). *After* being separated from his loving father and family and forced to live in a foreign land. *After* enduring false accusations, which led to his subsequent arrest and imprisonment. *After* all these events occurred, Joseph ascended to a position of authority and power.

The New Testament's records of the life and ministry of Jesus Christ draw our attention to examples of patience while enduring adversity. In John 5, we read of the man with an infirmity so debilitating he was unable to move about freely for thirty-eight years. Our reflection on Day 13 spoke of the Woman with the issue of blood in Mark 5 who, for twelve years, endured physical pain and misery. Her illness forced her to live on the fringes of society, where it appears she became accustomed to being overlooked, ostricised, and existing without a voice.

What's noteworthy is that neither person allowed their illnesses to be a paralysing force; instead, they sought out assistance in their attempts to be healed. After exercising their faith by speaking and reaching out to the Divine, each finally received relief. Their long period of suffering ended when Jesus Christ healed them.

These Biblical stories remind me that faithfulness is a beneficial gift. Being patient is not always easy, but the heavy load of waiting becomes lighter when coupled with faithfulness. My faith enables me to lean on what I do not understand, confident in the Almighty's promise that the best is yet to come!!!

I pray your faith allows you to trust God's promises. I've discovered the benefits and importance of continuing to spend time in God's presence. By doing so, each of us matures, and the Blessing of Spiritual fruits will be received.

Activity

Identify your Spiritual gifts. Write them down.

_____

_____

_____

Record those gifts you feel you are lacking.

_____

_____

_____

What have you done to attain these gifts?

_____

_____

_____

Prayer

Loving God, it is easy to become accustomed to instant gratification. Forgive me when I expect you to provide immediate results. Forgive me when I am impatient or when I do not demonstrate self-control. Teach me how to emulate your merciful, gracious, and patient manner. Amen.

Day #17

Oh May I See To

Fully Comprehend

Proverbs 14:29 NIV, "Whoever is patient has great understanding, but one who is quick-tempered displays folly."

James 3:13-18, NRSVUE, [13] "Who is wise and knowledgeable among you? Show by your good life that your works are done with gentleness born of wisdom. [14] But if you have bitter envy and selfish ambition in your hearts, do not be arrogant and lie about the truth. [15] This is not wisdom that comes down from above but is earthly, unspiritual, devilish. [16] For where there is envy and selfish ambition, there will also be disorder and wickedness of every kind. [17] But the wisdom from above is first pure, then peaceable, gentle, willing to yield, full of mercy and good fruits, without a trace of partiality or hypocrisy. [18] And the fruit of righteousness is sown in peace by those who make peace."

Reflection

One Sunday a few years ago, before the pandemic, I left church with the final hymn playing repeatedly in my head. I heard it as I walked into the parking lot to the vehicle and drove a short distance to the store. Walking the aisles and gathering my items, it replayed in my head. I continued to hum as I joined the line to cash out.

I was so engrossed in the song I neglected to observe what was happening around me. I did not realise the line was at a standstill until I heard those waiting demonstrate their impatience. My humming ceased as I focused on attempting to understand what was happening. Peeking towards the front of the line at the cashier, I saw a young lady with her head down. She was rummaging through her handbag, feverishly looking for something.

In her trolley were two girls who appeared oblivious to what was happening. The oldest was around five or six years of age. My quick assessment of the situation was that the line was at an impasse because the young lady needed additional funds to cover her bill. The cashier did not look bothered. However, the waiting customers had grown impatient. They were letting others know through loud sighs of disgust and shuffling of feet.

Instead of doing the same, I sought to put myself in this woman's shoes and attempted to understand what she was feeling at that moment. I could only imagine the embarrassment that I would feel. I then considered plausible options, including returning some items and having them voided from the bill. Recognising this option was not taken, I assumed every item was necessary. Grabbing the cashier's attention, I mouthed, "How much?"

The cashier held up a lone finger. The frantic search was undertaken in an attempt to yield a single dollar. I went to the cashier, paid the dollar, and returned to my spot in the line. As the cashier closed her sale, the woman looked at me and mouthed her appreciation.

During our everyday activities, there are often opportunities to assist others. Such opportunities are not always clearly identifiable, yet we can understand and assist when we are in tune with our surroundings.

Being of assistance often requires us to be willing to take ourselves out of our way to gain a better understanding. Are you prepared, ready, and willing to help? God is more than able to expand our understanding when we ask. We have an open invitation to request the Spirit of Understanding, which shall be granted to us.

Activity

Understanding - What does this Word mean to you?

_____

_____

_____

Do you think you demonstrate understanding in your everyday life?

_____

_____

_____

If so, write down one or two examples of how you demonstrated understanding recently.

_____

_____

_____

If you do not think you demonstrate understanding regularly, write down steps you plan on taking to becoming a more understanding person:

_____

_____

_____

Prayer

Yahweh, you have extended an open invitation to me to approach you. Answer my call, oh Lord, to gain sufficient understanding today. Allow me to move beyond my current way of thinking and being as I yearn to understand the needs of others. Open my eyes to see how I can be of assistance. Amen.

Day #18

Praise the One From Whom All Courage Flows

Deuteronomy 31:7-8, NIV, *7* *Then Moses summoned Joshua and said to him in the presence of all Israel, "Be strong and courageous,*

....

8 *The LORD himself goes before you and will be with you; he will never leave you nor forsake you. Do not be afraid; do not be discouraged."*

Reflection

Moving to a new place and beginning a new life takes a lot of courage. Anyone who has relocated understands it is quite an undertaking. There are many questions to be answered - how do I choose a community to live in that fits my family's needs? Which school is the best fit for the children? There are many aspects to consider - which service provider will connect the cable, or where can I find a reputable hairdresser?

There is also an emotional component associated with leaving all that is familiar and venturing into a new place. Many things will be different and unknown. I experienced all of these emotions and many more when I relocated to enroll in academia.

One afternoon, I went to the store to purchase a few food items before collecting my daughter from school. The plan was to return home, where we both would dive into homework and eat dinner at some point. God had other plans. As I exited the store, raindrops began to fall lightly. By the time I reached the vehicle, the rain was pouring down.

I flung my items in the car, put the key in the ignition, and turned it. Nothing. Fear slowly crept in as I turned the key a second time. Not only did the vehicle not start, but no light appeared on the dashboard, nor did the engine rev. Regardless of what I tried, the car did not start. I sat momentarily, gathering my thoughts as I did not know what to do or who to call. I felt alone. In the heavy downpour, I got out and walked around the parking lot looking for assistance.

I asked three different people for help. No one came to my rescue. Dejected, I returned to the car. I leaned on the steering wheel and cried out. I reminded God that I was obedient, having left *everything* I knew behind. I was here doing what was commanded of me. At that moment, I needed to know that I was not forsaken. I needed to feel and see the presence of the Divine move in my immediate situation.

I sat for a few minutes before turning the key again. The vehicle was silent, but somehow I could feel a change. A calmness washed over me. A peace entered my inner being. After waiting a few more minutes, I turned the key, and the vehicle finally started!!! After a sigh of relief, I expressed my appreciation by saying a quick thank you to God and took off.

There will be those instances in life when we feel alone, downtrodden, or afraid. In those moments, we find inspiration in the words Moses spoke to the Israelites and Joshua. The words of Deuteronomy 31:8 remain relevant today! Be encouraged, and rest assured that Jehovah Nissi will be near us forever!

Activity

What biblical verses do you turn to for encouragement?

_____

_____

_____

Have you ever felt an emotion of dejection or hopelessness? Describe the time.

_____

_____

_____

When was the last time you felt an immense peace wash over you?

_____

_____

_____

What situation were you addressing?

_____

_____

_____

Prayer

Jehovah Jireh, you are mighty and fearless. Undergird me when I step out in faith to launch something new. When fear and doubt creep in, uphold me with your strong hands as you Bless me with the Spirits of Courage and Determination to journey into the unknown. Amen.

Day #19

Come Along and Read With Me

Isaiah 41:10, NIV, "So do not fear, for I am with you; do not be dismayed, for I am your God. I will strengthen you and help you; I will uphold you with my righteous right hand."

Reflection

Life can throw a lot at a person - family discord, health challenges, financial struggles, instability in a career or job, disappointments - the list can go on and on for days. Whatever situation may arise, I draw comfort in knowing that I can bury myself deep in the Word of God and freely access the wisdom, reassurance, and hope within. I would like to share a few verses of Holy Scripture which resonate with me.

The Book of Job serves me well when I need to be reminded that I am not the sole person in the world experiencing hardship and challenges. The following verses draw to mind how fleeting and uncertain life is.

Job 14:1-2, KJV, [1] *"Man that is born of a woman is of few days and full of trouble.* [2] *He cometh forth like a flower, and is cut down...."*

I often turn to the Book of Psalms for consolation, reassurance, and reinvigoration. Life may be uncertain, but the Triune God can guide, direct, and comfort me as I traverse through the different phases.

Psalm 27:1-2, NIV, [1] *" The LORD is my light and my salvation— whom shall I fear? The LORD is the stronghold of my life— of whom shall I be afraid?* [2] *When the wicked advance against me to devour me, it is my enemies and my foes who will stumble and fall."*

Psalm 34:1-3, NRSVUE, [1] *"I will bless the Lord at all times; his praise shall continually be in my mouth.* [2] *My soul makes its boast in the Lord; let the humble hear and be glad.* [3] *O magnify the Lord with me, and let us exalt his name together."*

Psalm 98:1, NIV, *"Sing to the LORD a new song, for he has done marvelous things; his right hand and his holy arm have worked salvation for him."*

I am reminded of how and where to gain strength. Our Creator God does not desire for us to be discouraged but rather to be uplifted. We should aim to move out of the lowly place of distress.

> *Habakkuk 3:18 - 19, NIV,* [18] *"....yet I will rejoice in the LORD, I will be joyful in God my Savior.* [19] *The Sovereign LORD is my strength; he makes my feet like the feet of a deer, he enables me to tread on the heights."*

The awesomeness of the Almighty shines forth in the Scriptures. Receive the offered assurance that victory has already been won!!!

> *John 16:33, NIV,* *"....In this world you will have trouble. But take heart! I have overcome the world."*

When feelings of uncertainty, disheartenment, or loneliness creep in, when you feel no one truly understands your present situation, or when you feel as if the pressures of the day are caving in on you, I urge you to be intentional about making time to read the Holy Bible and freely receive the power and peace extended to all who believe in the Triune God.

Activity

In your instances of feeling down, overwhelmed, or discouraged by the actions or inaction of others, what do you do to recharge?

_____

_____

_____

Which Scriptures resonate with you? Is there a particular genre of Scripture you lean on for constant support? Write down the biblical verses that you find to be most life-giving.

_____

_____

_____

Prayer

Yahweh, your Word is always timely and is the light that shines brightly through the darkest periods of my life. They are life-giving and encouraging. Words cannot express my deep appreciation for sharing your Great Wisdom and Comfort. May your protective love forever keep me safe from harm. Amen.

Day #20

Time To Hit The Pause Button

Psalm 46:10-11, NIV, [10] *"He says, "Be still, and know that I am God; I will be exalted among the nations, I will be exalted in the earth." [11] The LORD Almighty is with us; the God of Jacob is our fortress."*

Reflection

Refreshment. For the purpose of this day, I invite you to rest.

When I have had a challenging day or am addressing a difficult situation, I know where I need to go to clear my head and discern the next step. I am drawn to nature and the ocean's peace and tranquility. It is where I go to gain energy, be refreshed, and recharge after so much has been depleted. I greatly appreciate the freedom to inhale the fresh air laden with sea salt. I want to look at the vast ocean for as far as my eyes can see. Fully aware my naked eye is unable to capture its end.

I laugh at the seagulls squawking loudly around me. Watching them communicate with one another as they fly above my head in circular motions or play together on the sand. On a sunny day, I can see the sun's rays glistening on the water top. Alone, there where sand meets water, I pause. The aim is not to be consumed with contemplative thoughts. Instead, I choose to shift my mind away from the challenge. There, by the water, I pause to allow myself to be still, to be reinvigorated.

I remind myself to count my blessings, as Mummy taught me, one by one. Being thankful draws attention away from the moment and towards the One who has brought me through past difficulties. Through it all, irrespective of what is happening, I should not forget how worthy of praise our Lord is. Then, I realise that I should do nothing other than praise my God of yesterday while aspiring to be in the presence of Elohim today.

My vision is focused on the beautiful ocean scenery directly in front of me. Still, my thoughts are centered around the goodness of the Triune God. All within the context of giving thanks. I encourage you to also purposefully push the pause button on life. Irrespective of what is going on and what storm is raging around you, focus on the One who can walk you through each day. *"I AM..."* deserves all admiration, honour, and glory for past, present, and future mercies.

Activity

Take a moment to find a quiet space. Perhaps it is a special place in your home, garden, or favourite nature trail near a park or a body of water.

Look around. Be intentional about truly seeing what exists around you.

Make a few notes about what you can touch, see, hear, and smell.

_____

_____

_____

_____

_____

_____

Are you able to pause and be still in the place you have chosen?

_____

_____

_____

Explain what is so special about it and what makes it a place where you can be reinvigorated.

_____

_____

_____

Prayer

Thank you for allowing me the opportunity to be in your presence as I learn to be still. May I be ever open to recognising the mighty works of your Hand in every place I go. Thank you for your wisdom in uncertain times. May you spread the Spirit of Peace, passing all understanding into life's situations. Amen.

Day #21

Watch The Relationship Flourish

Job 12:7 - 16, NIV, [7] *"But ask the animals, and they will teach you, or the birds in the sky, and they will tell you;* [8] *or speak to the earth, and it will teach you, or let the fish in the sea inform you.* [9] *Which of all these does not know that the hand of the LORD has done this?* [10] *In his hand is the life of every creature, and the breath of all mankind.* [11] *Does not the ear test words as the tongue tastes food?* [12] *Is not wisdom found among the aged? Does not long life bring understanding?*

[13] *"To God belong wisdom and power; counsel and understanding are his.* [14] *What he tears down cannot be rebuilt; those he imprisons cannot be released.* [15] *If he holds back the waters, there is drought; if he lets them loose, they devastate the land.* [16] *To him belong strength and insight; both deceived and deceiver are his."*

Reflection

Walking into a pet store to choose a pet can be quite an experience. There are so many options to observe and select from. Hamsters are running on stationary wheels, and caged birds squawking loudly. I always like looking at the large tanks' multi-coloured, beautiful fish. I enjoy being in the company of dogs and adorable puppies with large, cute eyes. Like many other creatures, they require a lot of time, energy, and attention.

Between the vet visits for essential shots, spending time together when I come home from work, and creating just the right environment for sheltering outside. I have had a dog or two who were very selective eaters and didn't like some bagged dog food choices I brought home. I had to learn their preferences, which foods they would eat, and which were outright rejected.

Food is not the only necessity. Ensuring a constant supply of drinking water, setting up playdates with other dogs, ensuring baths were given, and maintaining the maintenance list. One dog took a liking to a particular treat. I would go out of my way to secure a constant supply to witness the dog's pure joy. Perhaps you know exactly what I speak of and can recall a comical story or special moment you have shared or are currently sharing with your pet.

Caring for a pet means you are committed to ensuring their safety and well-being. A special relationship develops through the time spent together. The longer you stay together, the more you understand each other. The deeper your relationship becomes.

Reflecting on the stories shared on Day Two, I believe God seeks to cultivate meaningful relationships with each of us. A relationship where we human beings can blossom into new thoughts of understanding and discernment. Forging such a long-lasting relationship involves an interest in doing that which is not a will for self but what is of God.

Just as it takes time to build a relationship with other humans or with adored pets, it takes time and work to intentionally foster a relationship with the One who created and loves us. As I live and grow through different phases and events in life, my relationship with God continues to evolve through it all.

I am not the same person today as I was ten, five, or even two years ago. Through it all, I have realised that God is ever-present and willing to converse with me anywhere - at home, in the car as I drive, as I walk to an appointment - and at any time. Take time to pause, self-reflect, introspect, and talk freely and openly with God. It will be time well spent!

Activity

Make a few notes about any topic you wish to discuss with God.

_____

_____

_____

What plans will you implement to intentionally spend time with God moving forward? Are you empowered to discuss your topics with the Almighty?

_____

_____

_____

Prayer

Lord, your care and concern for my life make living possible. I don't know how to make it through these incredible and challenging times without your love and support. I have much to learn and am willing to gain more in a relationship with you. Be with me as I seek to be drawn nearer to you. Amen.

Exodus 9:16, NIV,

*"But I have raised you up for this very purpose,
that I might show you my power and
that my name might be proclaimed
in all the earth."*

About The Author

Teruco F. Tynes Charles' diverse real-life experiences have paved the way for her trust and faith in the Triune God, which she seeks to share with others in this devotion.

Teruco spent her formative years watching faith in action while living with her grandaunt in the archipelagic nation of The Bahamas. She holds a Master of Divinity degree from Mercer University and earned her Bachelor of Science from the University of Georgia (GA), USA.

Raised in the Anglican faith and formerly active in a non-denominational church, Teruco was ordained at Peachtree Baptist Church in Atlanta, GA. Her ministerial services include providing spiritual care to survivors of a catastrophic hurricane and being a hospital chaplain during the pandemic.

Proud Mom to Ari, Teruco enjoys trying new cuisine with her husband, Surish. She savours quiet, reflective moments by the beach.

www.ingramcontent.com/pod-product-compliance
Lightning Source LLC
Chambersburg PA
CBHW060421090426
42734CB00011B/2391